# COUNTRIES IN OUR WORLD

# SUDAN
## IN OUR WORLD

*Ali Brownlie Bojang*

A+

**Smart Apple Media**

Published by Smart Apple Media
P.O. Box 3263, Mankato, Minnesota 56002

U.S. publication copyright © 2011 Smart Apple Media.
International copyright reserved in all countries. No
part of this book may be reproduced in any form
without written permission from the publisher.

Printed in the United States of America at Corporate
Graphics, in North Mankato, Minnesota.

Published by arrangement with the Watts Publishing
Group Ltd., London.

Library of Congress Cataloging-in-Publication Data

Bojang, Ali Brownlie.
  Sudan in our world / by Ali Brownlie Bojang.
    p. cm. -- (Countries in our world)
  Summary: "Describes the economy, government,
and culture of Sudan today and discusses Sudan's
influence of and relations with the rest of the world"-
-Provided by publisher.
  Includes bibliographical references and index.
  ISBN 978-1-59920-434-5 (hardcover)
 1. Sudan--Juvenile literature. I. Title.
 DT154.6.B65 2011
 962.404'3--dc22
                            2009052421

Produced by: White-Thomson Publishing, Ltd.

Series consultant: Rob Bowden
Editor: Sonya Newland
Designer: Amy Sparks
Picture researcher: Amy Sparks

**Picture Credits**
**Corbis:** Cover (Penny Tweedie), 8 (Michael Freeman),
9 (Michael Freeman), 10 (Michael Freeman), 18
(Khaled ElFiqi/epa), 21 (Michael Freeman), 22 (Zhai
Xi/XinHua/Xinhua Press), 29 (Mohamed Nureldin
Abdalla/Reuters); **Dreamstime:** 7 (David Snyder),
23 (Condortre), 25 (Philip Dhil); **Getty:** 11 (Robert
Caputo/Aurora); **Photoshot:** 12 (World Pictures),
13 (Everett), 16 (WpN), 19 (UPPA), 27 (Xinhua);
**UN Photo:** 5 (Tim McKulka), 6 (Tim McKulka), 14
(Tim McKulka), 15 (Shereen Zorba), 17 (Fred Noy),
20 (Fred Noy), 24 (Evan Schneider), 26 (David
Manyua), 28 (Tim McKulka).

1207
32010


9 8 7 6 5 4 3 2 1

# Contents

*Sudan is the largest country in Africa and one of the poorest in the world. For more than 50 years, the country has suffered from famine and civil wars. Despite the problems in Sudan, though, its economy is growing rapidly, which may help improve the lives of its people.*

## Where in the World?

Sudan lies in northeast Africa. Although it is mostly landlocked, it has a 530-mile (853-km) border with the Red Sea. This is important for trade, because it means that ships can travel easily between Sudan and countries in the Middle East, such as Saudi Arabia. From there, goods can also be transported to rapidly developing countries, such as China and India, which need the resources Sudan exports. Sudan is also developing relationships with other African countries, particularly Kenya, partly through trade, and partly because of the movement of refugees.

▶ *Sudan has international land borders with the Central African Republic, Chad, the Democratic Republic of Congo, Egypt, Eritrea, Ethiopia, Kenya, Libya, and Uganda.*

### IT'S A FACT!

Sudan's name comes from the Arabic words *bilad al-sudan*, which mean "land of the black peoples."

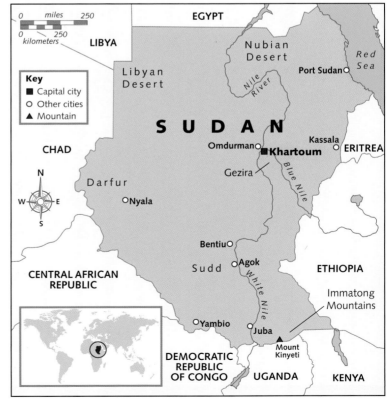

## Egyptian and British Influences

Since ancient times, the area that is now Sudan has had strong cultural and religious links with its northern neighbor Egypt, and at times the two regions were governed by the same leader. By the middle of the nineteenth century, Egypt had conquered almost all of Sudan, and the Egyptian leaders asked the British to help suppress revolts by the Sudanese people. In 1899, the Egyptians and British agreed to jointly rule Sudan. Until it achieved independence in 1956, Sudan was run as two separate colonies, the south and the north. This separation is thought to be one of the causes of political problems that later followed.

## North-South Conflict

The people in southern Sudan are mostly Christian or follow traditional beliefs such as animism, where everything in nature is thought to have a soul. The people in northern Sudan are mainly Muslims. When Sudan became independent in 1956, people in the south were concerned that the Muslims in the north would start to control the country. Two civil wars—in which different groups of people within a country fight each other—followed, with devastating consequences. Many people died and even more fled to other countries. A peace agreement was reached in 2005, but many people fear that this peace will not last.

▼ *People in Juba, the capital of southern Sudan, take part in a march on the International Day of Peace, September 22, 2008.*

## The Discovery of Oil

Oil was discovered in southern Sudan in the late 1970s. It has made some people very wealthy, but these are mainly people who are associated with the government in Khartoum (in the north), and foreign oil companies. Ordinary people living in the oil-producing areas have often been moved out of their homes and off their land to make way for the new oil fields. They are now poorer than ever. This was another cause of conflict between the people of southern Sudan and the government.

◀ *Although this oil field lies in Bentiu, southern Sudan, most of it is owned by foreign companies, so the Sudanese people do not benefit from the money made by extracting and exporting the oil.*

## Darfur

In 2003, fighting began in a region of Sudan known as Darfur. This is a very large area—about the size of Texas. People were angry that the government had done nothing to help them become less poor. During the fighting, thousands of civilians were killed or made homeless following attacks on villages. These attacks were often carried out by groups of men on horseback known as the *Janjawid*, who were supported by the government. In 2009, it was estimated that around four million people in Darfur needed help in the form of food and shelter, and that two million people—a third of the region's population—had been forced out of the area to other parts of Sudan or to neighboring countries.

## What Does the World Think?

Sudan is one of the most troubled countries in the world. The United States, the European Union, and the African Union have all pressured the Sudanese government to end the attacks in Darfur. They are particularly concerned because so many civilians have suffered. The United Nations claimed that the Sudanese government may have committed crimes against humanity and war crimes in Darfur, and ordered that the president of Sudan, Omar al-Bashir, be arrested and put on trial at the International Criminal Court. However, it is unlikely that this will happen since there may not be enough evidence against him.

 *A woman who has been forced from her home by the fighting sits with her child in a makeshift tent in a camp in eastern Darfur.*

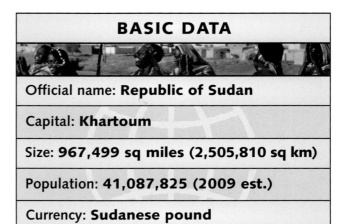

| BASIC DATA |
| --- |
| Official name: **Republic of Sudan** |
| Capital: **Khartoum** |
| Size: **967,499 sq miles (2,505,810 sq km)** |
| Population: **41,087,825 (2009 est.)** |
| Currency: **Sudanese pound** |

# Landscapes and Environment

*Sudan is the tenth largest country in the world, and the largest on the African continent, covering eight percent of its surface area. It is just over a quarter of the size of the United States. The landscapes vary across this huge country, and include deserts, mountain ranges, swamps, and rain forests.*

## The Shape of the Land

Most of Sudan is a vast, flat plain, but there are mountains and hills on the eastern, southern, and western borders. Mount Kinyeti, in the Immatong Mountains near the border with Uganda, is the highest point in Sudan, at 10,456 ft (3,187 m).

▼ *In the north, sandstorms, known as* haboob, *can completely block out the sun.*

## The Dry North

The north is very hot and dry, and temperatures can reach 118°F (48°C). The deserts here stretch across Egypt and Libya. Very few people live in this harsh region, but those who do are mainly nomadic tribes who travel around with their herds of goats and camels. There is a short rainy season from July to September, but in some places it does not rain at all.

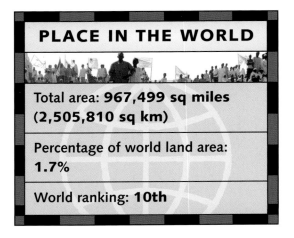

## PLACE IN THE WORLD

Total area: **967,499 sq miles (2,505,810 sq km)**

Percentage of world land area: **1.7%**

World ranking: **10th**

## The Tropical South

The south is also hot, but it has far more rainfall than other parts of the country. The rainy season lasts from June until November, and rainfall can be more than 39 in. (1,000 mm) a year. As a result, the landscape in this part of the country is made up of rain forests and swamps.

▼ *Women trample down a mound of cotton at harvest time in the Gezira project.*

## The Central Region

Central Sudan is open grassland. This land is ideal for farming if there is enough water. The central region is where most of Sudan's food for export is grown, although the main crop is cotton, grown in programs like Gezira.

## GLOBAL LEADER

### Irrigation

South of Khartoum, between the White Nile and the Blue Nile, lies one of the largest irrigation projects in the world—the Gezira. Small farms, known as *feddans,* are supplied with water from the Nile River through a series of ditches that total 2,672 miles (4,300 km) in length.

▲ *From the air, it is easy to see the point at which the Blue and White Niles meet, with strips of fertile land on either bank.*

## The Nile River

The Nile River is often called the "lifeblood" of Sudan. The two Niles, the Blue and the White, meet at Khartoum and flow north toward Egypt in a large, S-shaped curve known as the Great Bend. The Sudanese people rely on the Nile for most of their water needs, from drinking water to irrigating crops for food. Two thousand years ago, the Nubian Empire developed along the banks of the Nile in what are now Egypt and Sudan, because the river meant people could grow crops.

## IT'S A FACT!

The Nile River is the longest river in the world at 4,160 miles (6,695 km). Although the Nile carries water throughout the year, its depth and volume vary with the season, and during droughts, the Blue Nile can actually dry up. The White Nile is made up of many small tributaries, but about 94 percent of its waters are lost to evaporation before it meets the Blue Nile in Khartoum.

## Wildlife

Despite civil wars, there is still an abundance of wildlife in Sudan, particularly in the south. One of the largest movements of mammals—mainly antelopes and gazelles—have been recorded traveling along traditional migration routes in southern Sudan. Over 1,000 different bird species have also been identified in the same area.

## Environmental Threats

Sudan has many environmental problems. In the north, the deserts are advancing. People cutting down trees and overgrazing the land with goats and cattle have made this worse. Further south, the development of the oil industry has been responsible for damaging the habitats of some animals, such as elephants and zebras, and has led to a decline in their numbers. Oil pollution and the building of roads and pipelines have also led to a loss of fertile land.

## GLOBAL LEADER

### The Sudd

The Sudd is the largest area of wetland, or swamp, in the world. It occurs where the White Nile spreads out into an almost completely flat plain. It acts like a giant sponge, holding onto the waters of the White Nile and releasing them slowly throughout the year.

▼ *In the rainy season, the Sudd can increase to the size of the state of Mississippi.*

# Population and Migration

*There are about 20 different ethnic groups in Sudan. The main differences, however, are between the Arabic-speaking black Africans and Arabs, mainly in the north, and the non-Arabic-speaking black Africans in the south.*

**PLACE IN THE WORLD**

Population: **41,087,825 (2009 est.)**

Percentage of world total: **0.6%**

World ranking: **29th**

## Settlement in Sudan

Over the centuries, people from other African countries have settled in Sudan. Many of those in northern Sudan have strong links with other countries in North Africa and the Middle East, and are mainly Muslims. In the south, most people share their origins with people in East Africa and, in some cases, West Africa.

## Quality of Life

Most people in Sudan are very poor. Over half the population, and up to 90 percent in southern Sudan, live on the equivalent of less than one U.S. dollar a day. The number of children that die before they are five years old is 109 for every 1,000 births, and this is even worse in southern Sudan. This compares with eight in the U.S. and six in the UK.

▼ *A mosque in Kassala, northeastern Sudan. Most people in the north of the country follow the Islamic religion.*

## Ethnic Groups

The largest non-Arabic ethnic groups in Sudan are the Dinka and Nuer groups, who live in the south. These are made up of many different tribes and do not have a single leader, but the tribes have a common language and share similar traditions and beliefs. Both the Dinka and Nuer rely on raising cattle for their livelihood, and often move around to find the best land for grazing. They may grow crops in the rainy season.

Many Nuer and Dinka have left Sudan because of the civil wars. Some have moved to other African countries such as Kenya and Ethiopia, but the United States and Australia are also now home to thousands of Nuer and Dinka people.

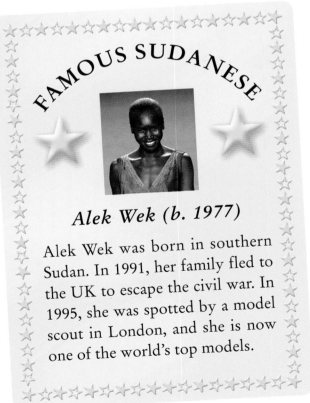

**FAMOUS SUDANESE**

### Alek Wek (b. 1977)

Alek Wek was born in southern Sudan. In 1991, her family fled to the UK to escape the civil war. In 1995, she was spotted by a model scout in London, and she is now one of the world's top models.

▶ *Alek Wek is from the Dinka tribe of Sudanese people from southern Sudan.*

## Refugees and Internally Displaced People

Since fighting broke out in Darfur in 2003, nearly two million people have left the area. Most of them settled in refugee camps, where they lived in makeshift shelters and relied on foreign aid for food and medical supplies. Some people traveled to towns and cities such as Khartoum, or even went to other countries in search of work. It was usually men who went, leaving the women behind.

◀ *These women were forced to flee from Abeyi, in central Sudan, because of fighting. They now live in Agok, in the south, where they rely on food rations from international aid organizations.*

## GOING GLOBAL

Sudan is badly affected by the emigration of skilled people, mostly doctors and other health professionals. It is estimated that out of 1,500 doctors who graduate each year, 800 leave the country to seek better opportunities in the UK and Ireland, as well as in Saudi Arabia and other Gulf countries.

## Fleeing to Sudan

At the same time that people were leaving Sudan, refugees fled to Sudan from conflicts in neighboring countries, such as Eritrea, Ethiopia, Uganda, and the Democratic Republic of Congo. In 2008, there were nearly 230,000 refugees in Sudan from other countries. Because the situation in Sudan is already very difficult, there are huge problems providing help for all these people.

▲ *A peacekeeping soldier from the joint United Nations-African Union*
*mission speaks with villagers in the war-torn region of Darfur.*

## Peacekeeping and Aid

The African Union (AU) is an organization of African countries set up to help one another in areas such as economic development and peacekeeping in troubled regions. As part of the AU, countries including Rwanda, Nigeria, and the Gambia have sent peacekeeping forces to Sudan. In addition, humanitarian aid has been sent to Darfur from all over the world, including the U.S., Europe, China, and Saudi Arabia. It has been very difficult for aid workers to travel around Darfur, though, because of the danger of being attacked by rebel groups. The World Food Program has provided an air service for foreign aid workers, flying them around the region, which is safer than traveling overland.

# Culture and Lifestyles

*Sudanese culture mixes the traditions and beliefs of all the many tribes that inhabit the country. These varied influences show in the religions, music, and fashions of the people in different parts of this large country.*

## Religion

Religion is a very important part of Sudanese people's lives. About 70 percent of the population is Muslim and these people are found mainly in the north, although groups of Muslims are found everywhere. Around five percent of the population follows Christianity, which was introduced in Sudan by missionaries in the nineteenth century. Many others follow traditional beliefs such as animism, where they believe that everything, including plants and rocks, has a soul. They often hold these beliefs alongside their Muslim or Christian beliefs.

▶ *Some people became Christians as a result of European missionaries traveling to Sudan. These boys are receiving religious instruction at a Catholic mission.*

## The *Souk*

At the heart of every Sudanese town is the *souk,* or market. These are lively, noisy places where craftspeople make and sell glass beads, wood carvings, leather bags, and saddles for horses and camels. Food and other household goods are also available to buy at the souks.

▲ *Soccer is very popular in Sudan. All over the country, people will get together for a game.*

## FAMOUS SUDANESE

### Manute Bol
### (b. 1962)

Manute Bol, from southern Sudan, became the tallest man ever to play in the National Basketball Association (NBA) league in 1985. He originally wanted to play soccer, but he soon realized that at 7 ft. 7 in. (2.31 m) he was too tall, so he turned to basketball, where his height was a big advantage.

## Sports

Many sports are popular in Sudan, including traditional wrestling and horse racing, and at the 2008 Beijing Olympics, Sudan won its first-ever medal—silver in the men's 800 meter run. Soccer is the most popular sport, however, and is played all over the country. The Sudanese national soccer team is nicknamed *Sokoor Al-Jedian*, or Desert Hawks. Even in remote villages, children get together for a game. Fans support their favorite teams, but they also eagerly follow the leagues in England, Spain, and Italy.

## Family Life

As in many Arab and African societies, the family is important and highly valued. Families are usually large, and often grandparents, aunts, uncles, and cousins all live together. The most important person in the family is usually the oldest man, but sometimes it may be the oldest woman. The Sudanese have traditional views about the different roles of men and women. Women are expected to look after the home and the children, and they do not often go out to work.

## Hospitality

Sudanese people put great value on welcoming people into their homes, whether they are friends or strangers. Food and drink are served, and the guest is very well looked after. A sheep may be slaughtered (killed) for dinner for important guests. Meals are usually eaten from a large communal bowl using the right hand, a spoon, or a piece of bread. The Sudanese have a very special way of preparing coffee, where they fry the beans and grind them up with spices.

▼ *Sudanese people believe that cooking and looking after the children are the women's responsibilities.*

## Education

School is free and compulsory between the ages of 6 and 14, but many children in the countryside find it difficult to go to school. Their schools may have been bombed, they may not be able to afford to buy books and uniforms, or they may need to stay at home to work. During the civil war in southern Sudan, only one percent of girls completed their primary-school education. Many schools in Darfur have been destroyed during the conflict.

▲ *Children at a school in Yambio, southern Sudan. Although all children are supposed to attend school until they are 14, war has prevented many of them from keeping up their education.*

## IT'S A FACT!

Internet use is increasing in Sudan, with a ratio of 37 for every 1,000 people having Internet access in 2007, compared to 0.9 in 2000. The number of cell phones is 20 times greater than the number of landlines in Sudan.

## Music

Many different kinds of music are popular in Sudan, although the strongly Islamic government does not approve of modern music. Some musicians have even been imprisoned; others have left Sudan so that they can play their music freely. This has helped spread Sudanese music around the world.

# Economy and Trade

*In the past, farming was the way most Sudanese people earned a living. Even today, 80 percent of the population work the land. Oil is now helping to improve Sudan's economy, and the oil industry is providing jobs for more Sudanese.*

## Livestock and Crop Farming

The type of farming people do depends on where they live. In the north, people look after herds of animals, moving from place to place to find the best land for grazing.

Further south—where higher rainfall makes it easier to grow crops—there are settled farms, where farmers grow grains, such as sorghum, millet, and wheat, as well as vegetables.

▼ *A farmer in Nyala harvests the cereal crop sorghum. He was given the seeds by the Food and Agriculture Organization of the United Nations, as part of an international program to help farmers.*

## GOING GLOBAL

Sudan's major trading partners include China, Japan, Saudi Arabia, South Africa, India, the UK, Germany, Indonesia, and Australia. The relationship with China is particularly important, as it is one of the fastest-growing economies in the world, and trade agreements with China can bring in a lot of money to countries like Sudan.

▶ *These workers are loading sacks of sesame onto a freighter ship, for export to countries such as China and Egypt.*

## Producing to Export

Sudan produces many crops for exporting to other countries, but the main one is cotton. There are several fair-trade cotton projects in Sudan, where workers are given a fair wage and where some of the money earned by selling the cotton is invested in the community—for example, in health care or schools. Fair-trade goods are very popular in other countries. Sudan is Africa's third largest producer of sugar, after South Africa and Egypt. Sudan also exports sesame, groundnuts (peanuts), gum arabic, and livestock, as well as natural gas, gold, silver, and many other mineral resources.

## Oil—Black Gold

Oil was discovered in Sudan in the 1970s. Several foreign companies were interested in working in Sudan to exploit the oil, but were forced to abandon their plans because of the wars. However, oil is now Sudan's main export and although the country does not produce as much as Nigeria or Angola, production is increasing rapidly. Sudan produces around 500,000 barrels of oil a day, which earn the country about US$7 billion a year. The income from oil helped Sudan's economy grow at an average rate of nine percent a year until the recent economic crisis. This was a higher rate than many industrialized countries.

▲ *This Chinese farmer is showing a Sudanese man how to sort cucumbers at a Chinese-run farm near Khartoum.*

## GOING GLOBAL

Many Chinese people have come to Sudan as construction workers in the oil and building industries. They have brought aspects of their own culture with them and have started their own basketball league. In Khartoum, there is a supermarket stocked with Chinese produce that is flown in from China every week.

## China's Special Role

China's economy is growing so rapidly that it needs raw materials for its factories and food for its booming population. It has developed strong relationships with many African countries that produce oil, minerals, and food products in order to meet these needs. Sudan is one of the most important providers of raw materials, and China buys over 80 percent of Sudan's exports. This may be affected by the global economic crisis that began in 2008, though. China's economy has suffered, and this may have a domino effect on Sudan. China has also invested a lot of money in construction. For example, it has built a pipeline from the oil fields to Port Sudan and a tanker terminal at the port.

## Khartoum Develops

In contrast to much of the rest of the country, the city of Khartoum is booming. The oil industry has attracted many foreign businesses, and since 2000, new factories, shopping malls, hotels, and office blocks have been built, as well as a new airport. The condition of existing roads is improving, and more are being built. There are far more cars now than there were just a few years ago.

▼ *Modern hotels like this one in Khartoum reflect Sudan's booming economy.*

## IT'S A FACT!

Sudan is the seventeenth fastest growing economy in the world and the fourth fastest in Africa. It rose by nine percent between 2006 and 2007, which is a much higher rate than most industrialized countries. This is largely because of its oil exports. As oil runs low in other countries, countries like Sudan, which have reserves of oil, can sell the oil at a good price.

## Poverty in the Rural Areas

Despite the boom in Khartoum, there is still widespread poverty, particularly in the rural areas. It is estimated that four out of every 10 children are underweight, and most villages still lack roads, electricity, and proper drainage facilities. Many people in rural areas still have to walk long distances to draw water from wells.

*Sudan is an independent Islamic republic. The country is governed by a small group of Muslim clerics or brotherhoods based in the capital, Khartoum. However, large parts of the country are beyond the control of the government.*

## IT'S A FACT!

The conflict between north and south Sudan, which began in 1955, is the longest civil war in African history.

### The Government

In 1989, Omar Hassan al-Bashir overthrew the Sudanese government, backed by the military. In 1993, he became president of Sudan. Until that time, the different regions of Sudan had enjoyed some level of self-government, but al-Bashir took away that power and put it all in the hands of a central government in Khartoum. He introduced Islamic law, known as *Sharia,* throughout the whole country, even for people who were not Muslims. No one was allowed to oppose the government—those who did were sent to prison. Newspapers were not allowed to print what they wanted.

◀ *President al-Bashir (right) meets with the Secretary-General of the United Nations, Ban Ki-moon, in 2007 to discuss the crisis in Sudan.*

▲ *Thousands of Sudanese gathered to celebrate the opening of the Merowe Dam, on the Nile near Khartoum, in March 2009.*

## Sudan and Its Neighbors

The introduction of *Sharia* law in Sudan caused concern for some of the country's neighbors. They were afraid that it would spread into their own countries. In the 1990s, Uganda, Kenya, and Ethiopia joined together to try to stop the spread of *Sharia* law, and they were supported by the United States. Relationships between Sudan and these countries have been poor ever since, and they have accused each other of supporting rebel groups in each other's countries.

## The Nile Basin Initiative

Sudan has better relationships with its neighbors over the Nile River. Although there are sometimes disagreements, the countries work together to make sure they can all benefit from the Nile's waters. The Nile is vital to all the countries through which it passes, and an estimated 300 million people depend on it for domestic water supplies (for washing and drinking), as well as for irrigating crops. These countries have formed an agreement, called the Nile Basin Initiative. Egypt, downriver from Sudan, has helped Sudan with dam-building projects and invested money in a canal-building project in the south to regulate the flow of water.

## A Terrorist State?

Since 1993, the U.S. has considered Sudan to be a country that supports terrorism. The U.S. government said that American companies were not allowed to do any business in Sudan. In 1998, it bombed a pharmaceutical factory in Khartoum because it was believed that chemical weapons were being produced there that might be used for terrorist activities. In 2001, the U.S. started to allow its companies to do business in Sudan once more, because it could not prove that the Sudanese were involved in terrorism.

▼ *These Nigerian soldiers are part of the United Nations-African Union Mission (UNAMID) in Sudan.*

### GOING GLOBAL

On November 17, 2006, former UN Secretary-General Kofi Annan announced that Sudan had agreed to allow the establishment of a joint African Union and United Nations peacekeeping force within its borders. This cooperation with an international organization was seen as a sign of Sudan's improved status in world affairs.

## A New Peace

In 2005, the north and south of Sudan reached a peace agreement. In this agreement, oil deposits were to be shared equally between the north and the south. Although still part of Sudan, the south was allowed to have some control over its own affairs. A date was set for 2011 for the two parties to decide if southern Sudan will stay as part of the country or separate and become independent.

▼ *Sudanese people gather to protest against the arrest warrant issued for President al-Bashir.*

## Holding Sudan Accountable

In December 2006, the International Criminal Court decided to bring a case against members of the Sudanese government. It believed some people had committed war crimes and had violated human rights in Darfur. In July 2008, President al-Bashir was charged with genocide for planning to kill all the people of Darfur's three main ethnic tribes, the Fur, the Masalit, and the Zaghawa. Although the court issued a warrant for his arrest, he has not yet been put on trial. Many people believe he never will be because there is not enough evidence against him.

# Sudan in 2020

*By 2020, southern Sudan may be an independent country—or it may remain united with the north as part of a stronger and more peaceful nation. If the 2005 peace agreement works, Sudan's economy may continue to grow. This could reduce poverty and improve the lives of the Sudanese people.*

## Sharing the Wealth

Oil has already made some Sudanese people very wealthy, and experts believe there is a lot more oil to be exploited in Sudan. However, it is important that the benefits of oil production are shared more equally among the country's people so the very poor members of the population can begin to rise out of poverty. If this does not happen, there may be further unrest and wars.

*▼ These children are searching a garbage dump in Juba for food and clothing. If life is to improve for the Sudanese people, the country's wealth must be shared more equally.*

◀ *Modern cars and Western-style advertising on the streets of Khartoum are signs of Sudan's improved economy.*

## Tourism in Sudan

The government knows that it cannot depend too heavily on oil. It cannot rely on the world market because oil prices go up and down all the time, and one day the reserves of oil will run out. Other industries must be developed to help the country prosper. If there was peace in the country and better roads and transport, tourism could play an important part in Sudan's future. It is an ancient country with a fascinating history, and there are many places of interest, including the ancient pyramids of Meroe, diving in the Red Sea, and the markets of Omdurman, that would attract visitors if they felt it was safe to travel there.

## Economic Prospects

Sudan could be a successful and prosperous nation. It has plenty of land available to grow crops, and enough water from the Nile to irrigate them. This means it could grow enough food for its population as well as for exporting to other countries, which would bring in much-needed money. For this to happen, the government needs to invest in the farming industry, such as setting up more irrigation projects. This would be a major step in helping the country toward a more stable future, where people in all parts of Sudan may enjoy an improved quality of life.

# Glossary

**animism**  the belief that spirits inhabit all natural objects, such as rocks and trees.

**Arab**  someone who belongs to a race of people that originated in the Arabian Peninsula. Arabs are usually Muslims and speak Arabic.

**civil war**  a war in which different groups within the same country or region fight each other.

**colony**  a country or a region that is under the political control of another country.

**continent**  one of the world's seven great land masses: Africa, Antarctica, Asia, Australia, Europe, North America, and South America.

**drought**  a prolonged period without rainfall.

**economy**  the financial system of a country or region, including how much money is made from the production and sale of goods and services.

**ethnic**  relating to a specific group of people with the same background.

**export**  to send or transport products or materials abroad for sale or trade.

**famine**  a serious shortage of food.

**genocide**  the systematic killing of a group of people, often because of their racial or cultural background.

**humanitarian**  the importance of promoting the welfare of people.

**human rights**  the basic freedoms to which everyone in the world is entitled according to the United Nations Universal Declaration of Human Rights (UDHR).

**International Criminal Court**  an international law court set up in 2002 as the world's first permanent war-crimes court.

**irrigation**  supplying dry land with water by means of ditches and channels in order to make it suitable for growing crops.

**nomad**  someone who has no permanent home and moves from place to place, often with livestock.

**refugee**  someone who has to flee from their home to another country because of war or persecution.

**republic**  a political system in which the head of state is an elected president rather than a king or queen.

**resources**  things that are available to use, often to help develop a country's industry and economy. Resources could be minerals, workers (labor), or water.

**terrorist**  a person who uses violence or causes fear to try and change a political system or policy.

**tributaries**  a smaller river or stream that flows into a larger river.

# Further Information

## Books

*Darfur: African Genocide*
by John Xavier
(Rosen Publishing, 2008)

*Genocide in Darfur*
by Janey Levy
(Rosen Publishing, 2009)

*Sudan*
Countries in Crisis
by Sean Connolly
(Rourke Publishers, 2008)

*Sudan*
Cultures of the World
by Patricia Levy and Zawiah
Abdul Latif
(Marshall Cavendish, 2008)

*Sudan*
Global Hotspots
by Geoff Barker
(Marshall Cavendish, 2008)

*Sudan*
Nations in the News
by Charles Piddock
(World Almanac Library, 2007)

## Web Sites

**https://www.cia.gov/library/publications/the-world-factbook/geos/su.html**
CIA World Factbook

**http://www.darfurchallenge.org/ resourcesforteachers.html**
Classroom resources for teaching about Darfur.

**http://www.sudanembassy.org/**
The Sudan Embassy web site, including information about the country, its people, history, and more.

*Every effort has been made by the publisher to ensure that these web sites contain no inappropriate or offensive material. However, because of the nature of the Internet, it is impossible to guarantee that the contents of these sites will not be altered. We strongly advise that Internet access is supervised by a responsible adult.*

# Index

Numbers in **bold** indicate pictures.